The AB Papers

First Published 2020

Published in the United Kingdom
in 2020 by The QB Papers

Design by Burgess Studio
Printed on Munken Pure Rough Cream
Printed in the UK by Principal Colour
Typeset in Garamond

ISBN 978-1-913119-01-0

Thirteen Things

Quentin Blake

The RB Papers

Banana

Useful Box

Sundial

Skateboard

Road Map

Rucksack

Bathing Hut

Suitcase

Magnifying Glass

Bird Book

Clothes Peg

Straw Hat

Heirloom

Banana

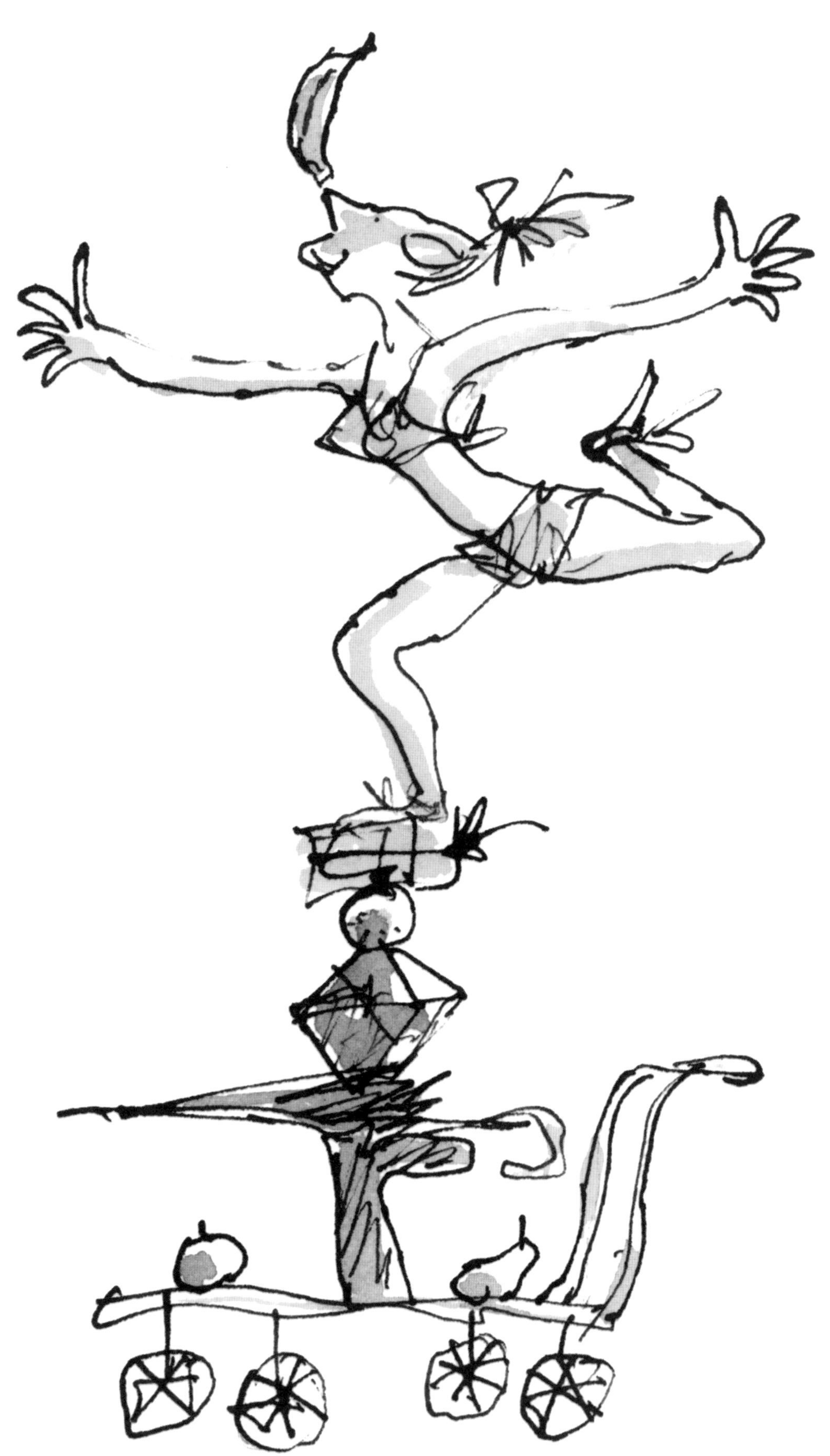

Useful Box

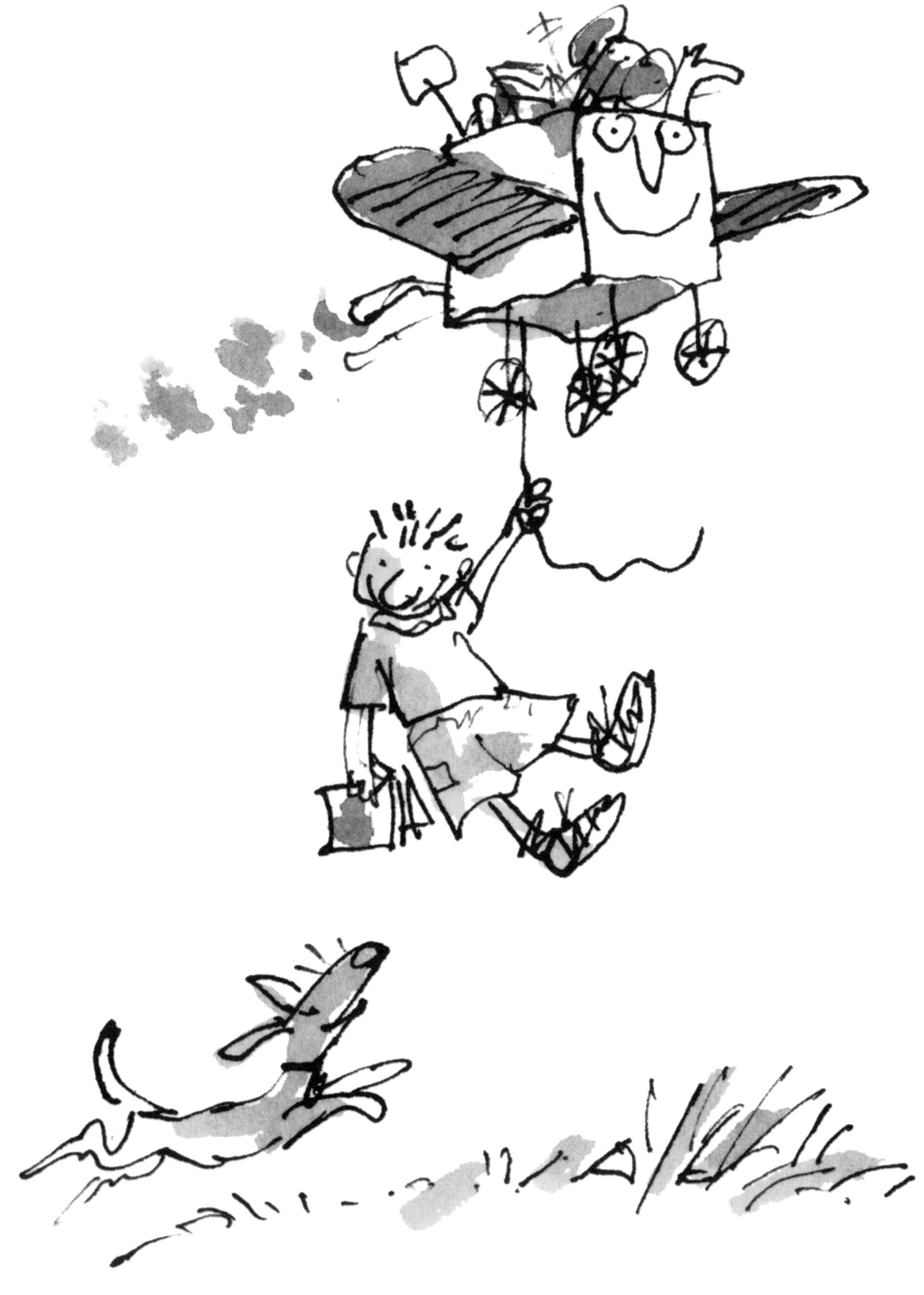

Sundial

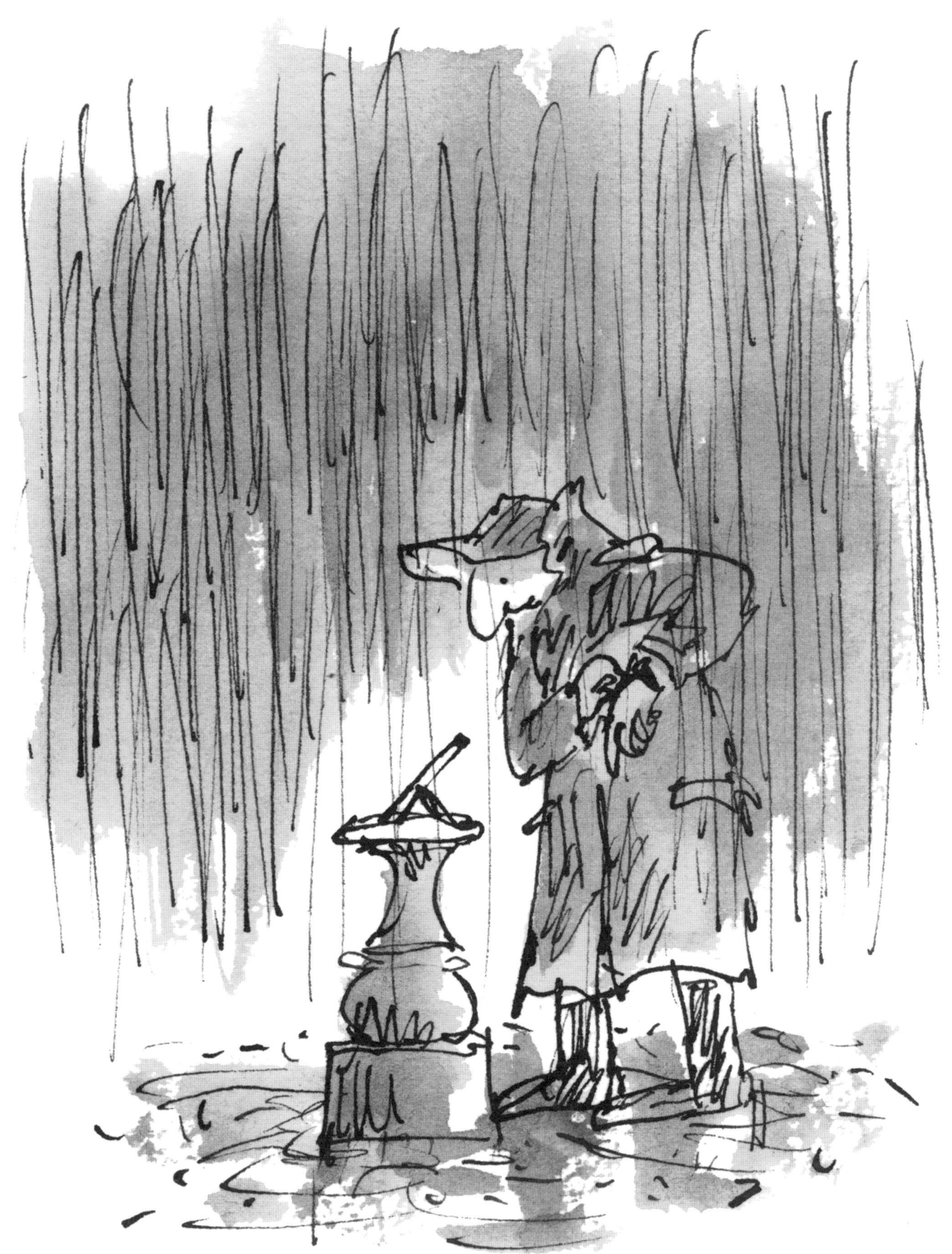

Skateboard

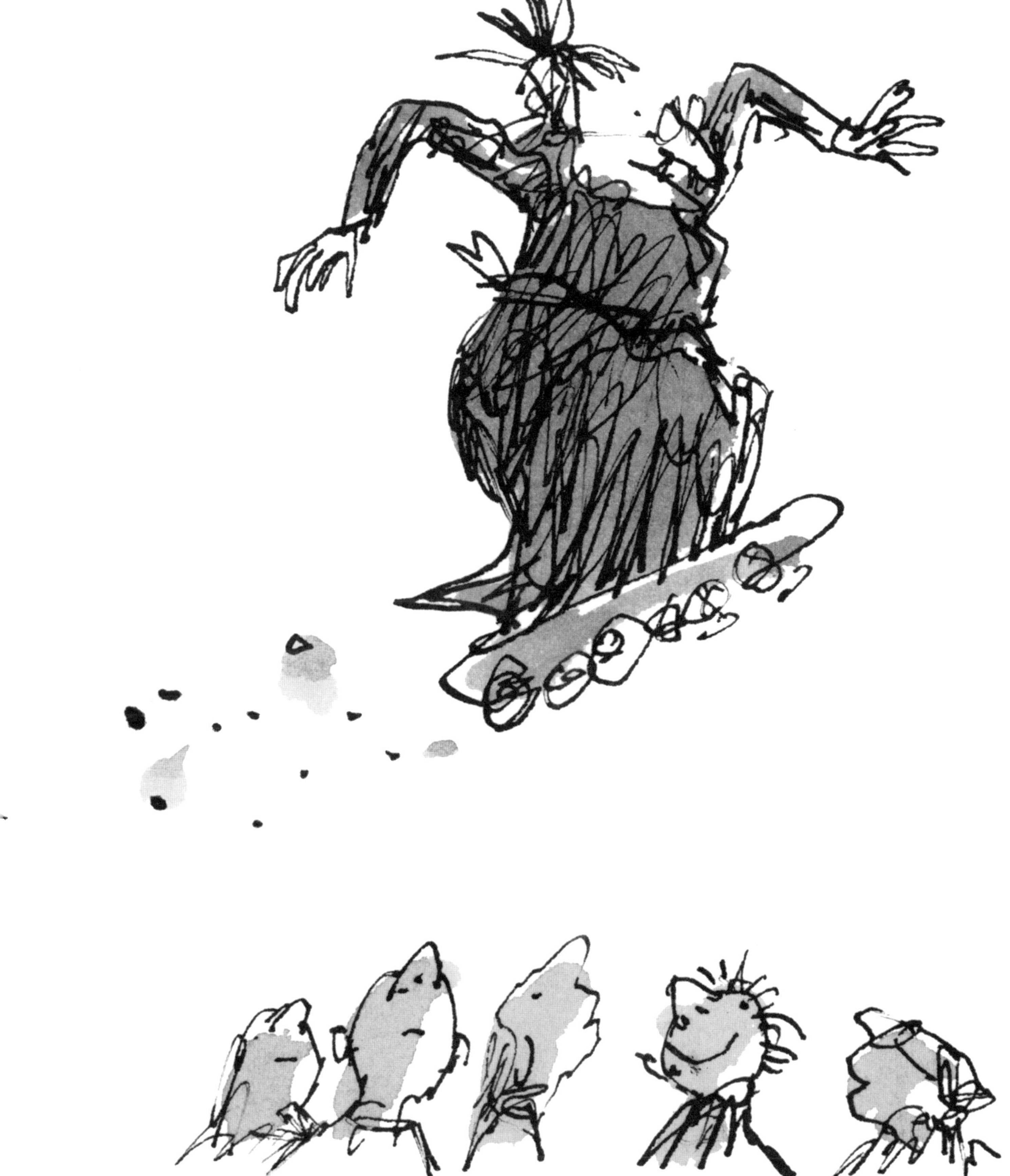

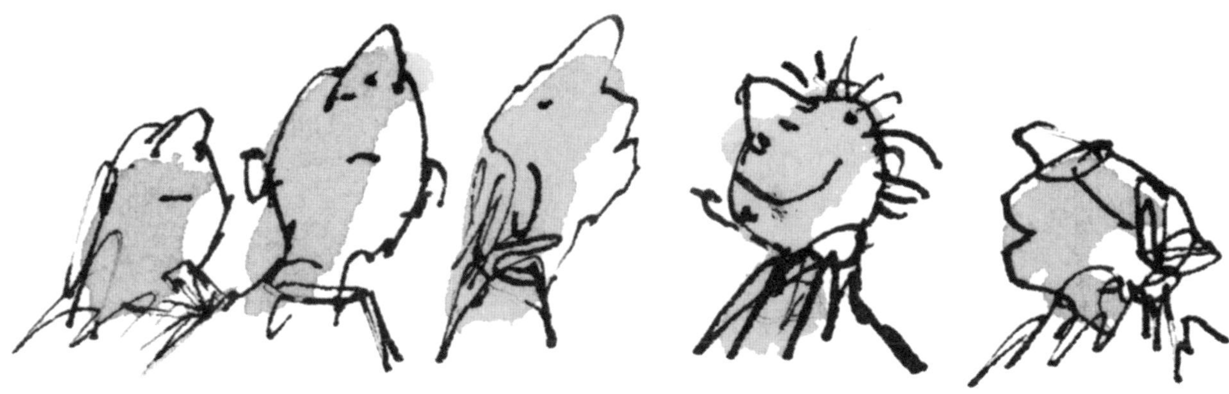

Road Map

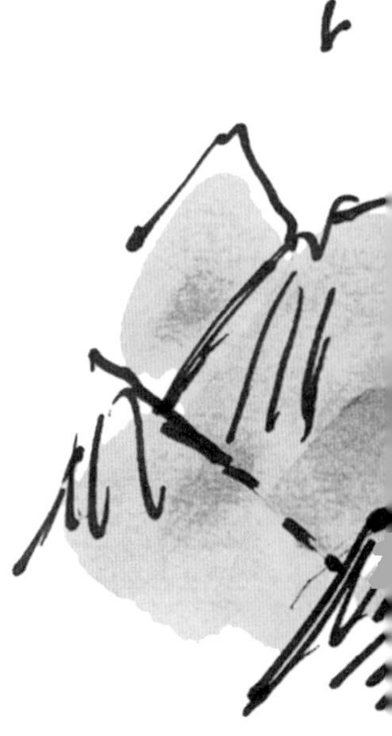

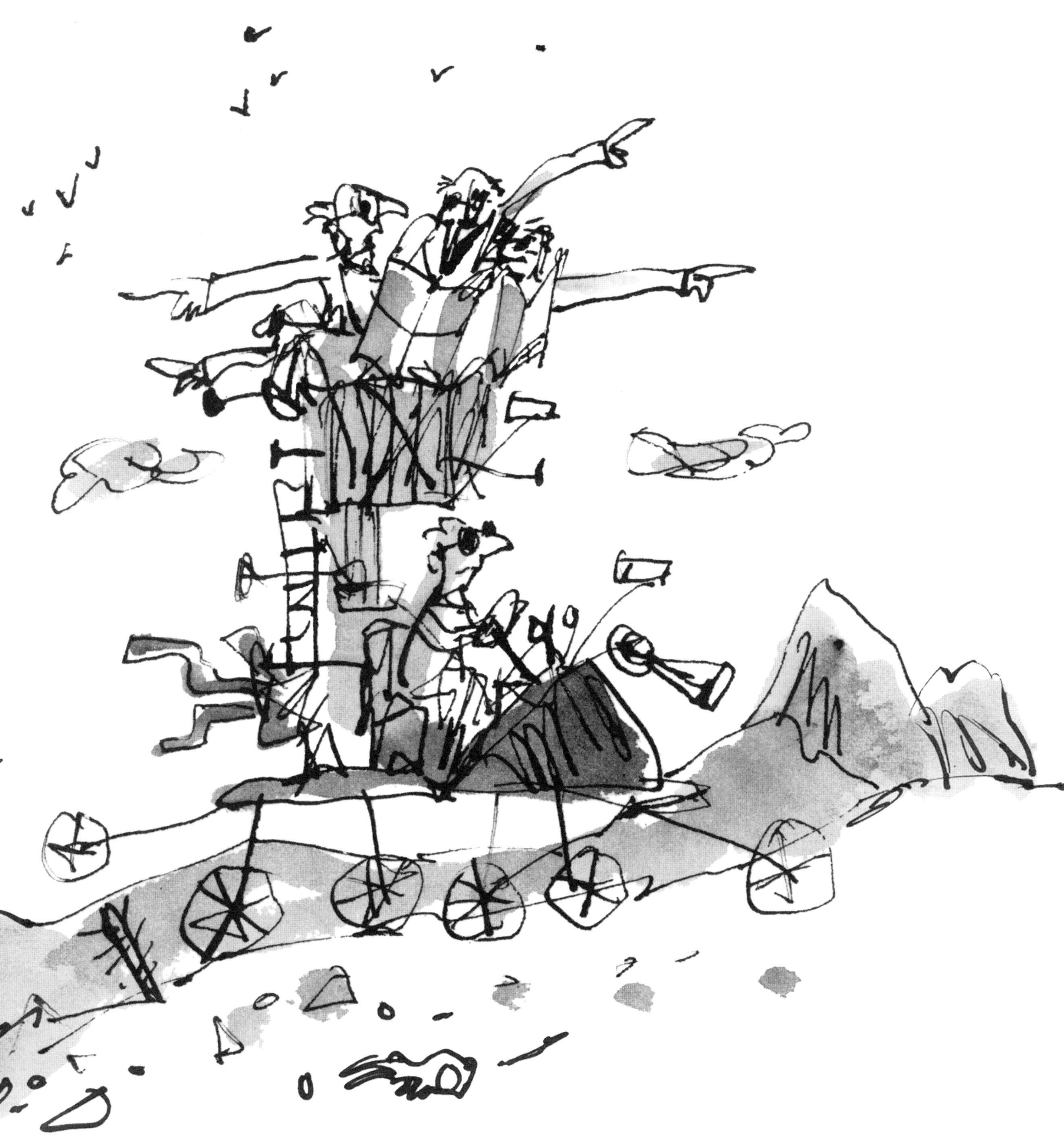

Rucksack

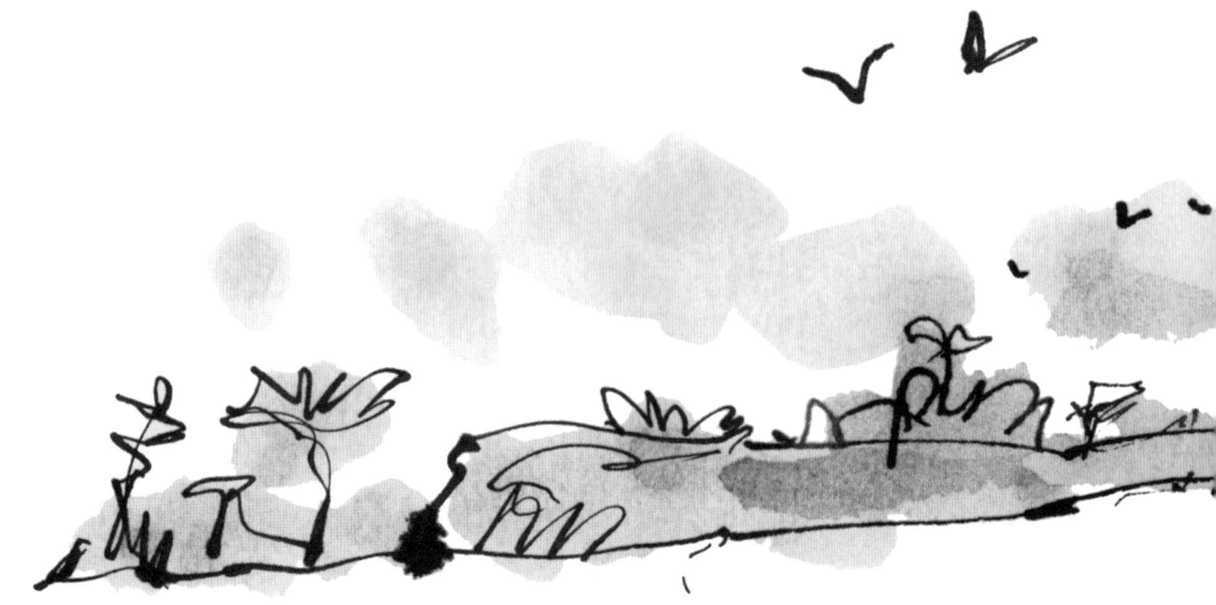

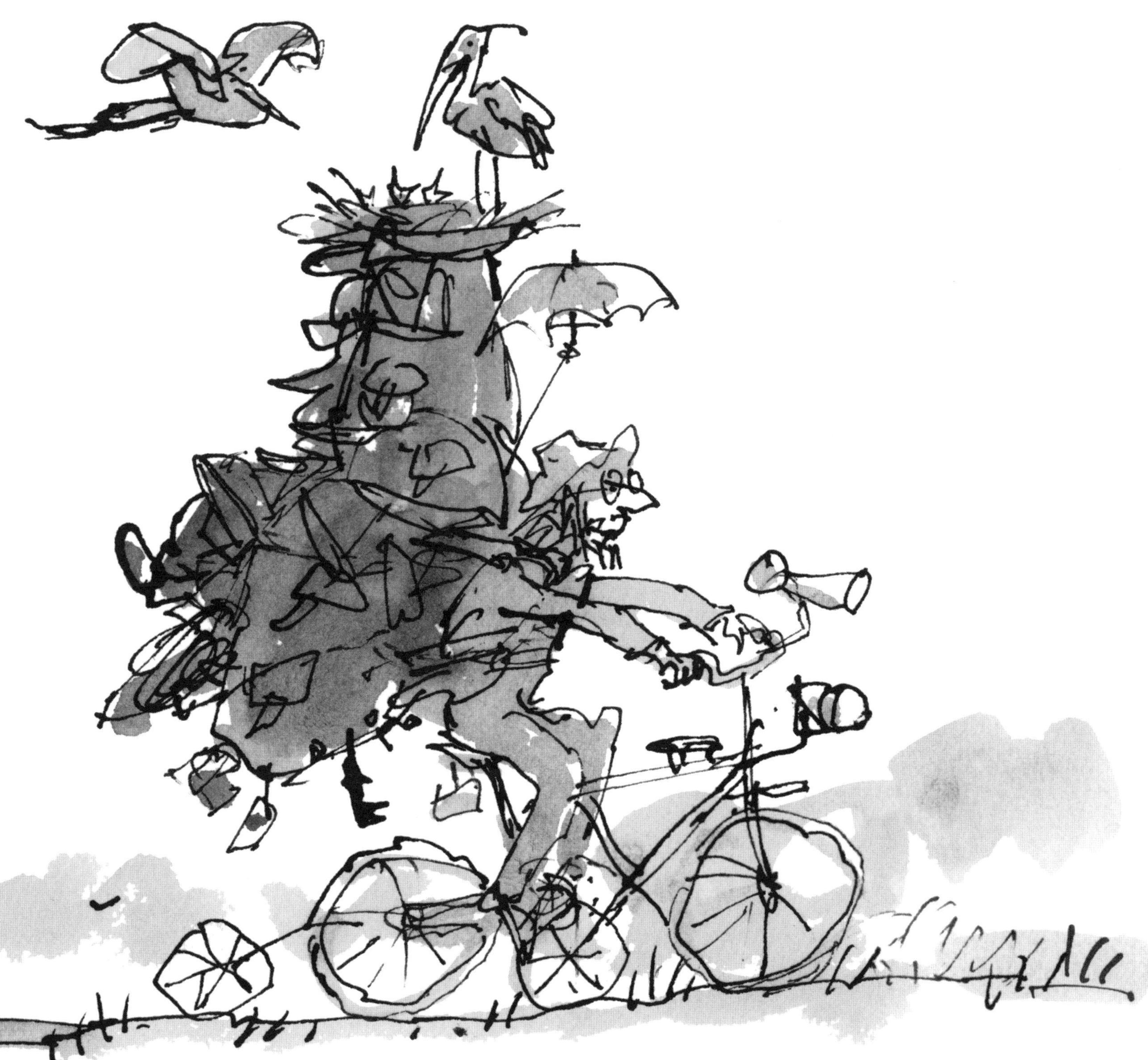

Bathing Hut

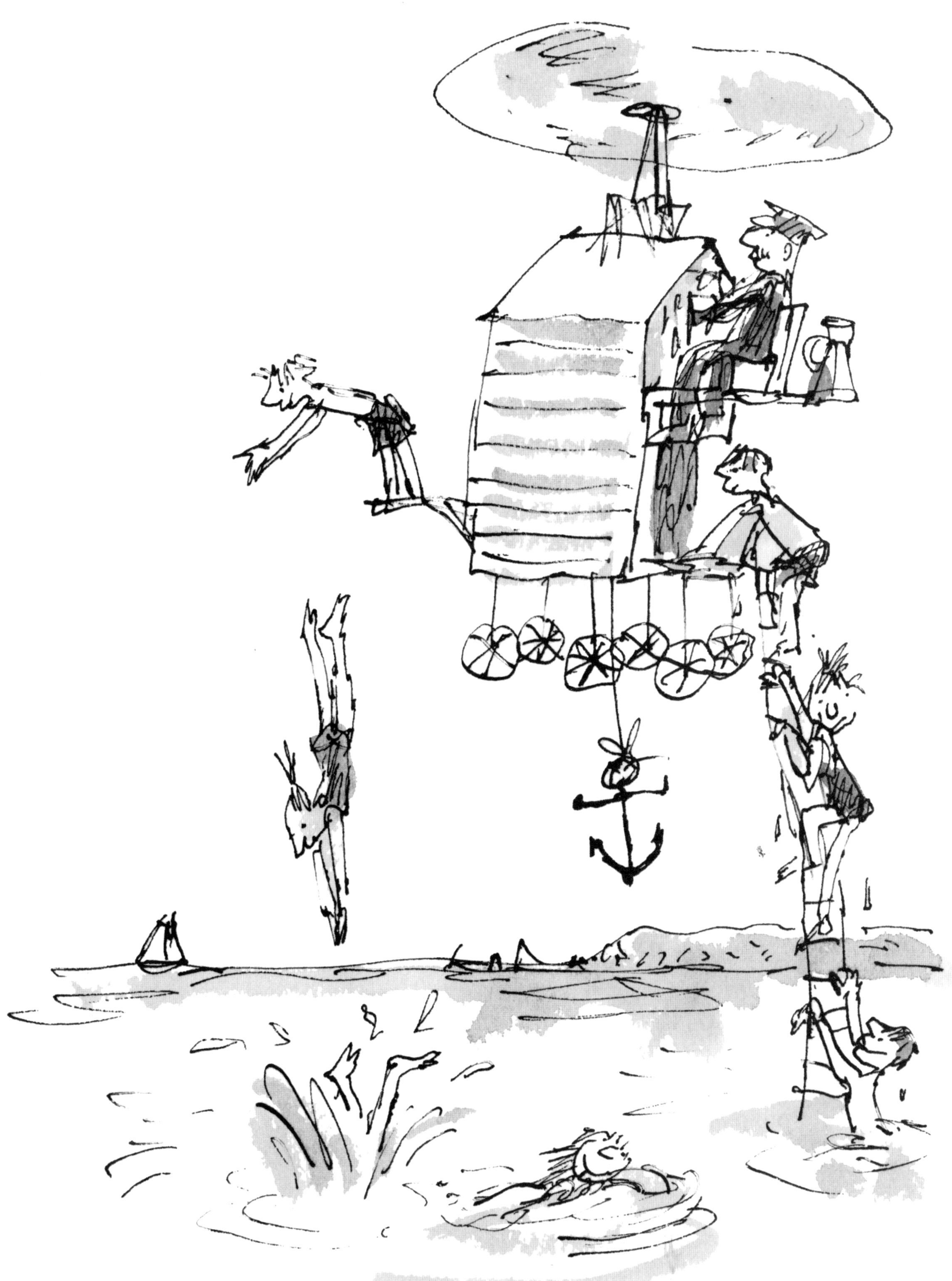

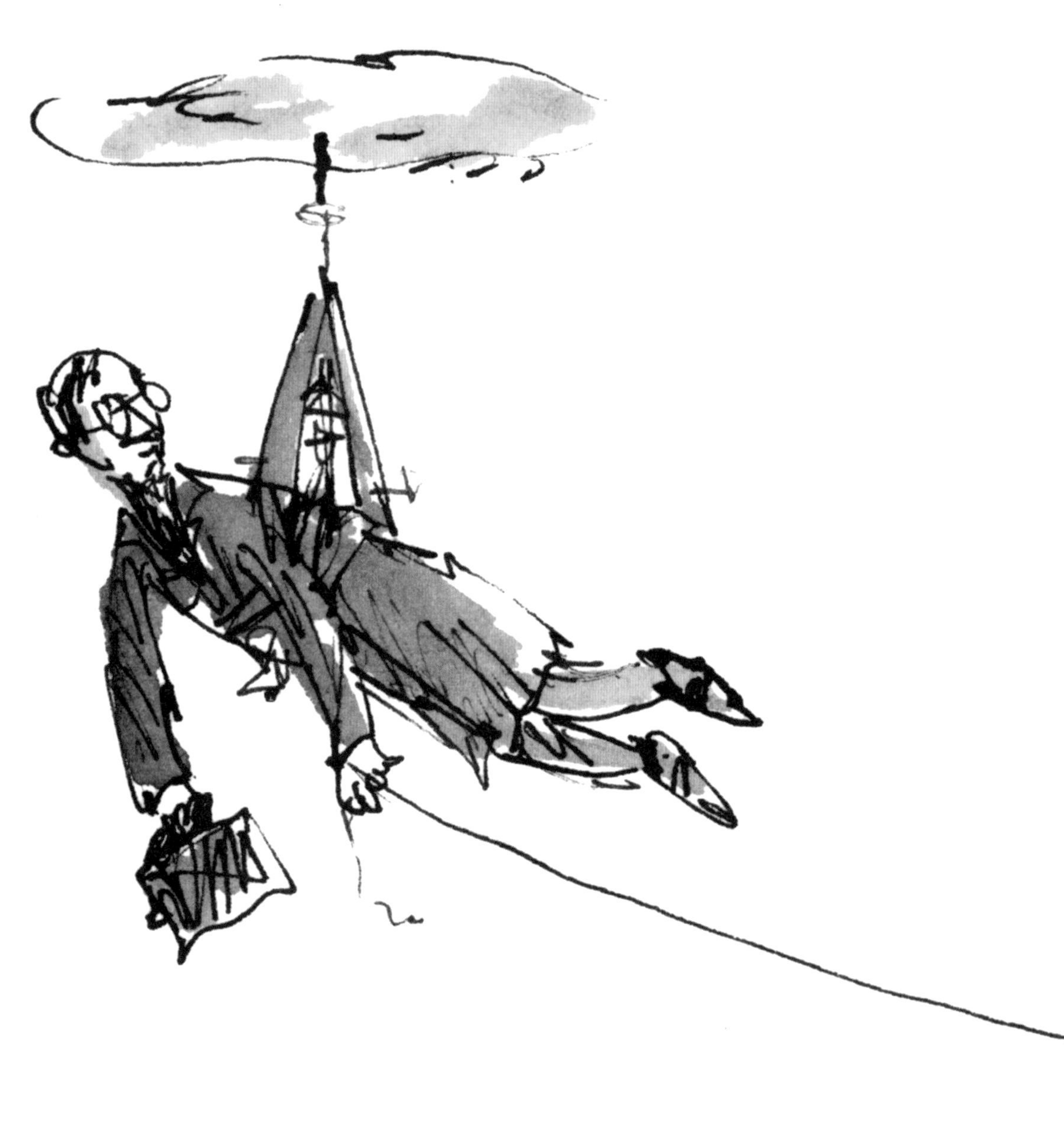

Suitcase

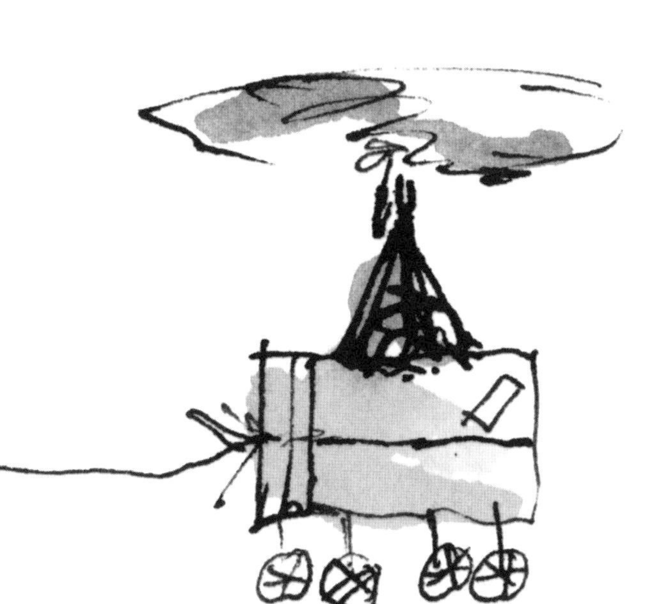

Magnifying Glass

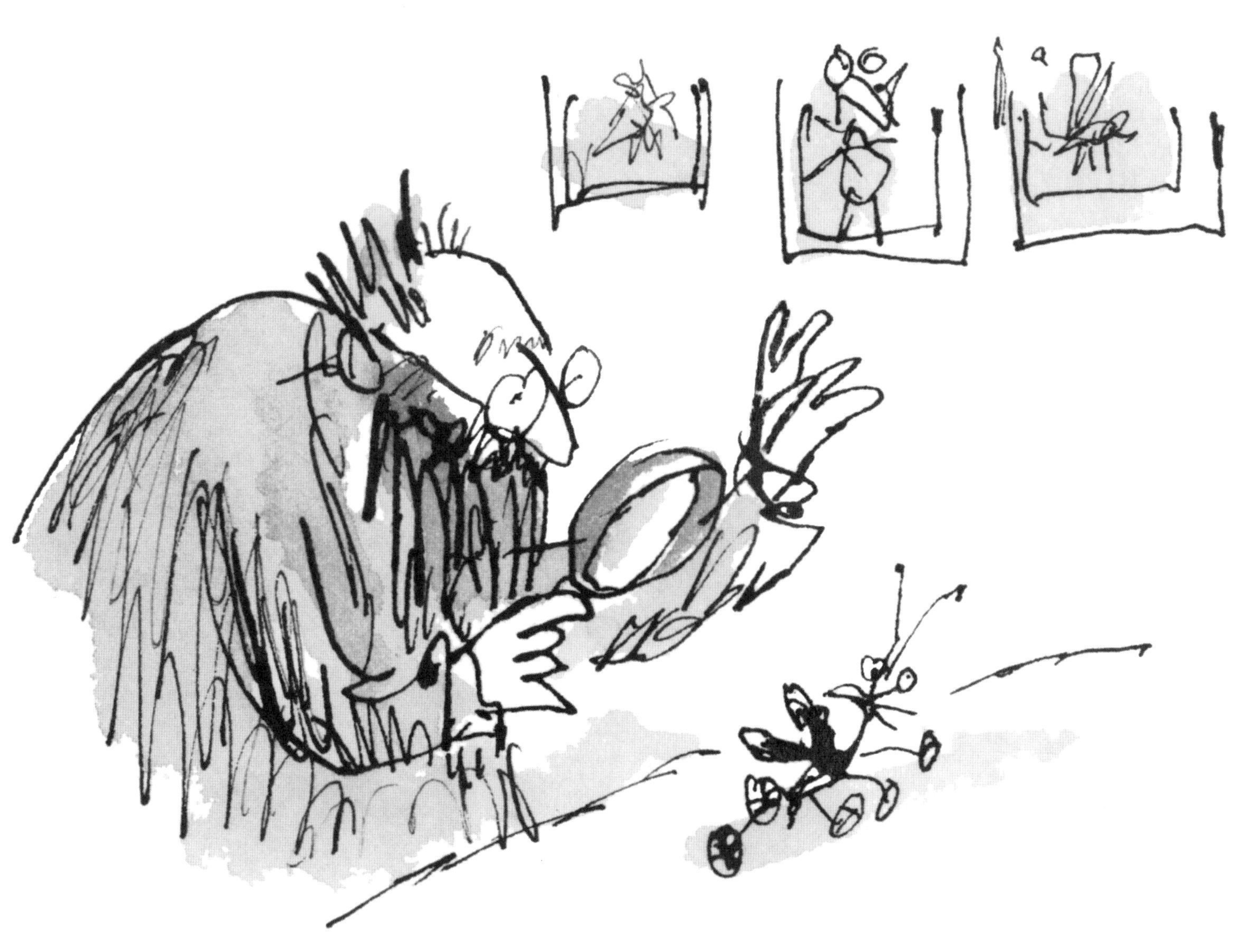

Bird Book

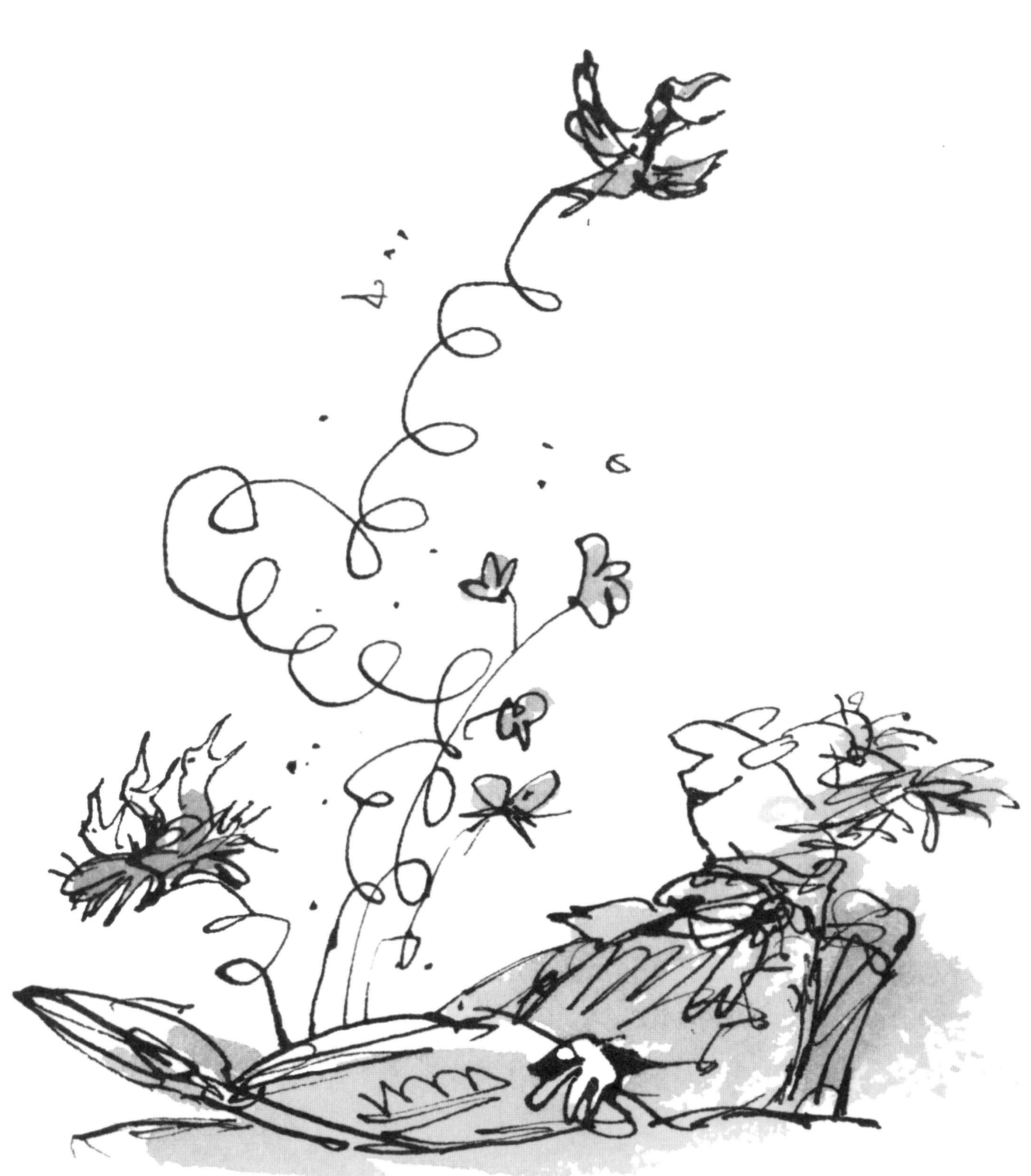

Clothes Peg

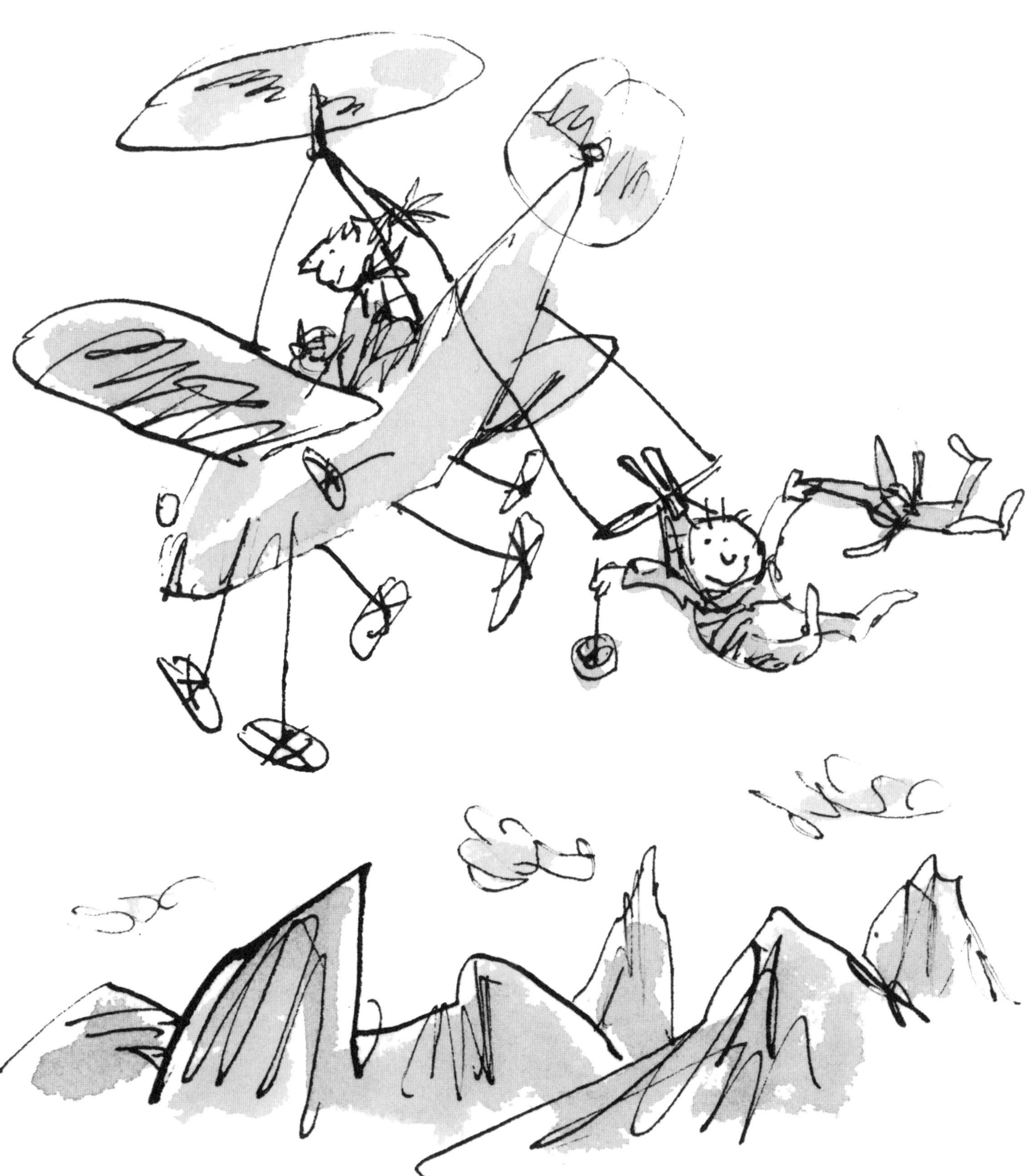

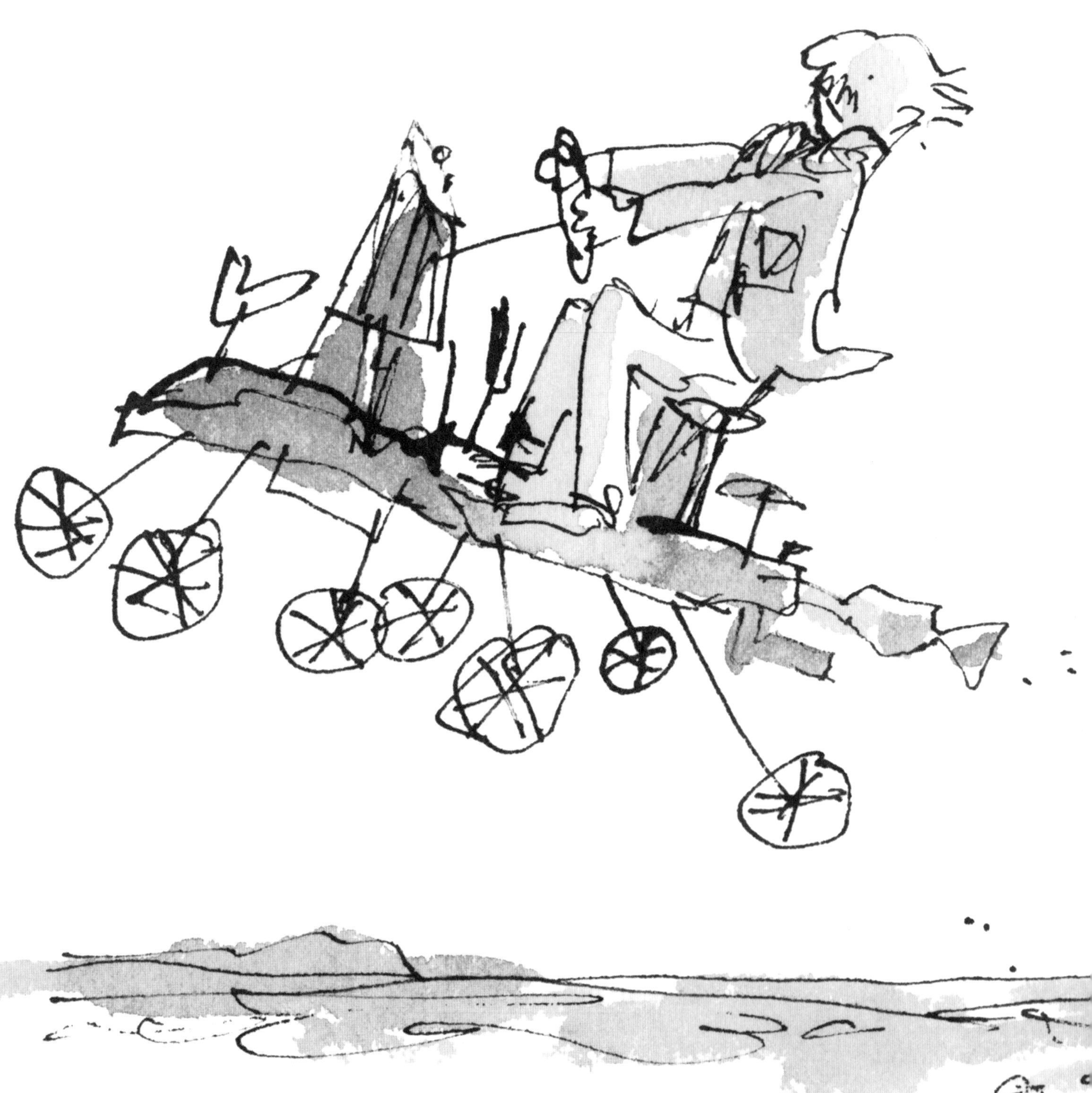

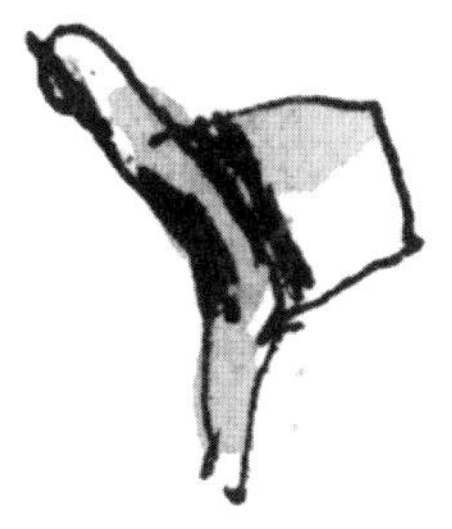

Straw Hat

Heirloom

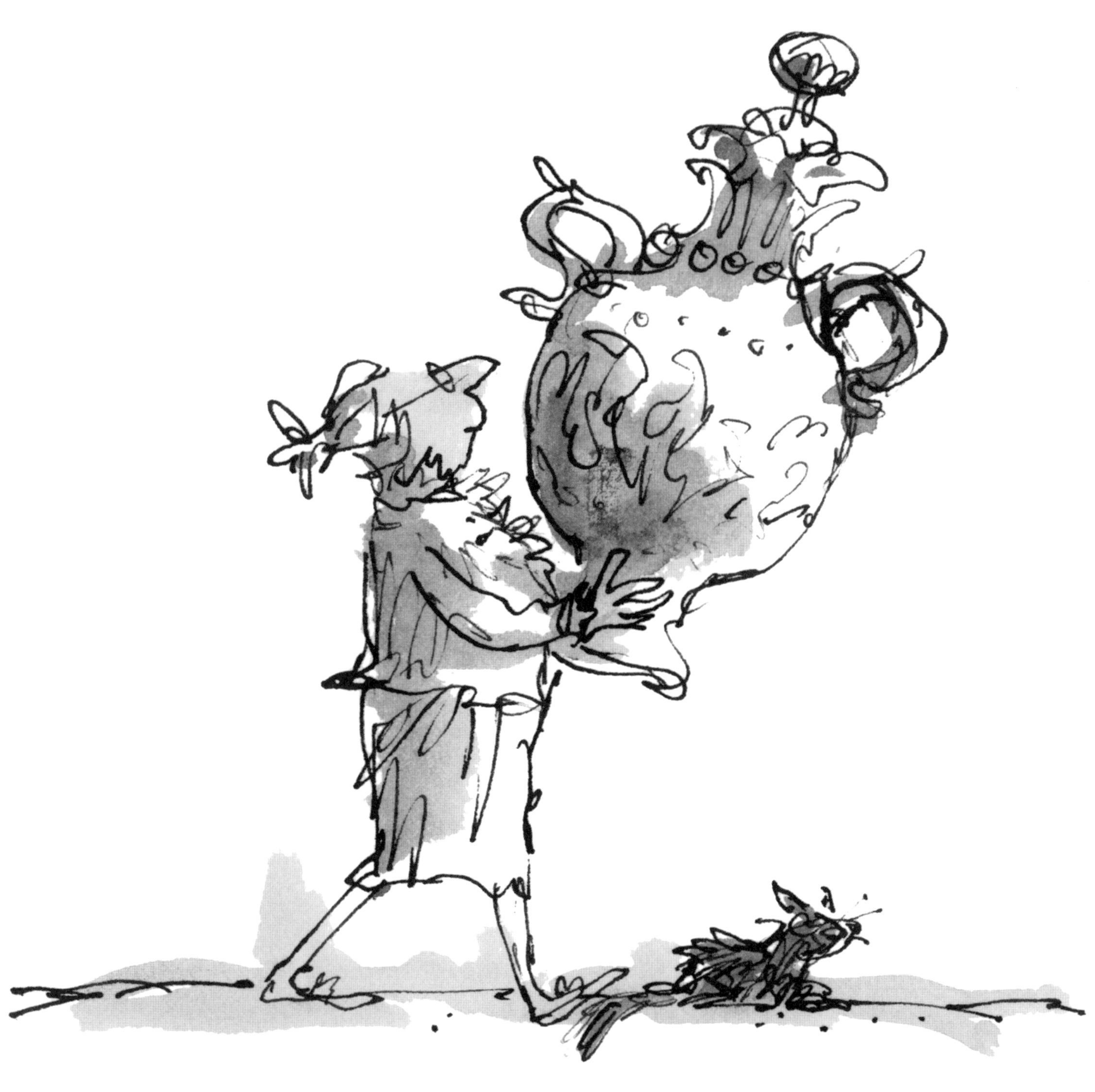